To my family.

*— J. L.*

## Selected Bibliography

Billings, John D. *Hardtack and Coffee; or, The Unwritten Story of Army Life.* Illus. Charles W. Reed. Lincoln, NE: Bison, 1993.

Burgess, Lauren Cook, ed. *An Uncommon Soldier: The Civil War Letters of Sarah Rosetta Wakeman, Alias Pvt. Lyons Wakeman, 153rd Regiment, New York State Volunteers, 1862–1864.* New York and Oxford: Oxford University Press, 1996.

Burns, Ken, dir. *The Civil War: 25th Anniversary Edition.* 2015; Alexandria, VA: PBS, pbs.org/kenburns/the-civil-war.

"Civil War Letters." National Postal Museum. postalmuseum.si.edu/research-articles/letter-writing-in-america/civil-war-letters.

Mansfield State Historic Site and Museum. Louisiana State Parks. lastateparks.com/historic-sites/mansfield-state-historic-site.

## Permissions

The images of Rosetta's letters included in this book have been created using scans of Rosetta Wakeman's original 1862–1864 letters, held by the Doane family. The author and publisher would like to thank Ruth Goodier and Jackson K. Doane, Jr., relatives of Rosetta Wakeman, for their work in sharing Rosetta's story.

The author and publisher would like to thank Lauren Cook Wike for the use of her edited transcripts of Rosetta Wakeman's letters, published as *An Uncommon Soldier: The Civil War Letters of Sarah Rosetta Wakeman, Alias Pvt. Lyons Wakeman, 153rd Regiment, New York State Volunteers, 1862–1864* (Oxford University Press, 1996). The transcripts retain Rosetta's original spelling and grammar, with ellipses marking where a quote has been shortened for *Guts for Glory*. Dates have been standardized for consistency.

Photo of Sarah Rosetta Wakeman and photo of Lyons Wakeman gravestone courtesy of Jean Lafitte National Historical Park and Preserve (@TradingCardsNPS) on Flickr.

Text and illustrations © 2024 JoAnna Lapati

Published in 2024 by
Eerdmans Books for Young Readers,
an imprint of Wm. B. Eerdmans Publishing Co.
Grand Rapids, Michigan

www.eerdmans.com/youngreaders

Manufactured in China

33 32 31 30 29 28 27 26 25 24      1 2 3 4 5 6 7 8 9

A catalog record of this book is available from the Library of Congress.

ISBN 978-0-8028-5464-3

Illustrations created with scratchboard and digital materials

Find a *Guts for Glory* discussion guide—including recommended reading lists for all ages and educational activities—through the Eerdmans Books for Young Readers blog (eerdlings.com/discussion-guides).

# GUTS FOR GLORY

The Story of Civil War Soldier ROSETTA WAKEMAN

*written and illustrated by* JOANNA LAPATI

Eerdmans Books for Young Readers

Grand Rapids, Michigan

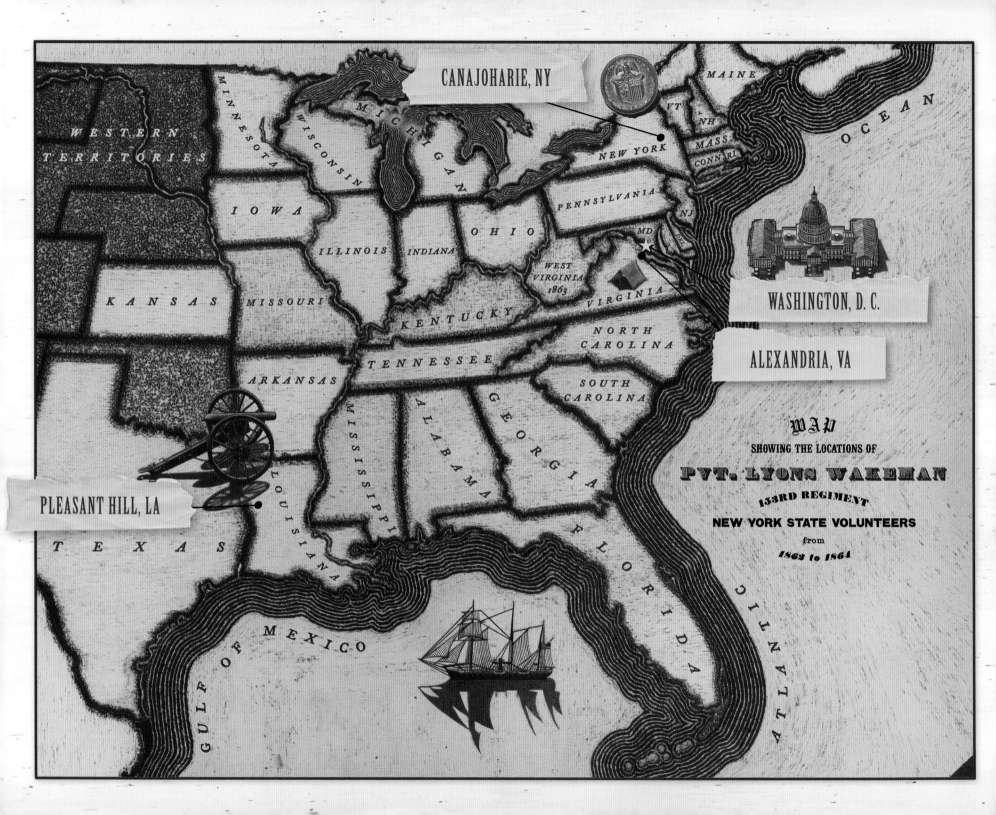

CANAJOHARIE, NY

WASHINGTON, D.C.

ALEXANDRIA, VA

PLEASANT HILL, LA

MAP

SHOWING THE LOCATIONS OF

PVT. LYONS WAKEMAN

153RD REGIMENT

NEW YORK STATE VOLUNTEERS

from

1862 to 1864

The war between the North and South showed no signs of stopping.
As men were called for duty, women remained on the home front.

In upstate New York, Rosetta Wakeman did her best to support her family day after day.

Every morning, she milked the cows stream by stream.

She ground the coffee crank by crank.

She mended her family's clothes stitch by stitch.

She dressed her siblings button by button.

But a life filled with chores soon became dull.

She wanted something . . . *different*.
She wanted something *more*.

So one night, when her family was asleep, Rosetta made a bold decision. She bound her chest, got dressed in her pa's old clothes, clutched a pair of shears in one hand, took a deep breath . . . and cut off her braid. Then she tiptoed out of the old, creaky house.

Outside, a breeze tickled her bare neck.

She practiced speaking in deep, low tones and pondered a name
for her new self. "Lyons Wakeman," she whispered.

By dawn, she sighted a coal barge several miles from her home.
Eager to try her disguise, she approached the boatmen.
"The name's Lyons Wakeman. You folks need a hand?"
"Can you steer a boat and help drive a team of mules?" asked the man.
"Yes, sir!"

Lyons joined the crew, transporting coal up along the Chenango Canal.

No one suspected her secret.

# $152 BOUNTY! $152

## TO ARMS! TO ARMS!

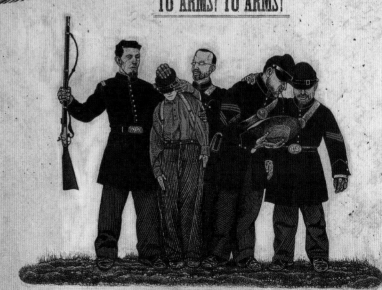

Several days later they reached the town of Canajoharie, where a huge crowd had gathered. The country was at war, and a new regiment was forming. Able-bodied men were signing up with the 153rd New York State Volunteers, eager to fight for the Union.

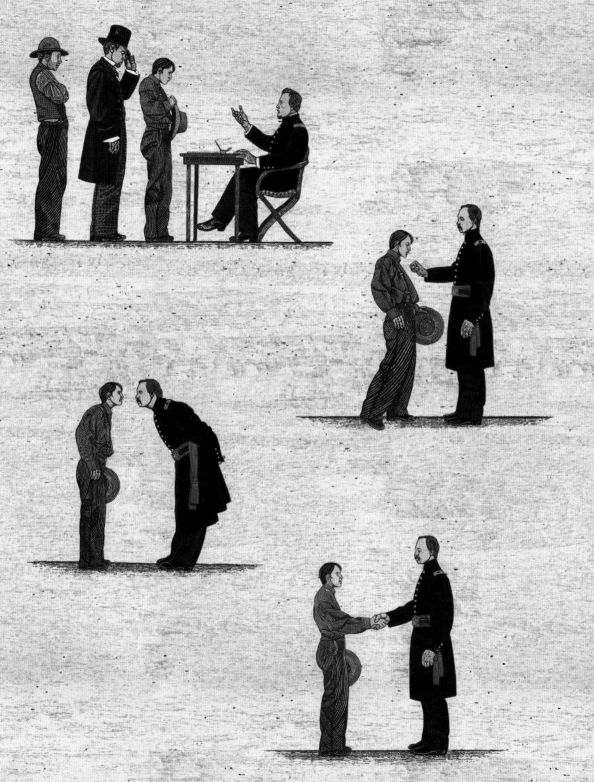

Lyons stepped toward the enrollment table. *Am I too young to enlist?* she wondered. She signed the roster, adding two more years to her age.

Next came the medical exam. Lyons gulped. *Will they discover I'm a woman?* But a thump to the chest, a glance at the teeth, and a firm handshake qualified Lyons fit for duty.

"I, Lyons Wakeman, do solemnly swear that I will bear true faith and allegiance to the United States of America . . ."

...bear true faith and allegiance to the United States of America...

The next day, the 153rd left their home state and headed toward Alexandria, Virginia, ready for duty.
Lyons stood proud in her newly issued uniform.

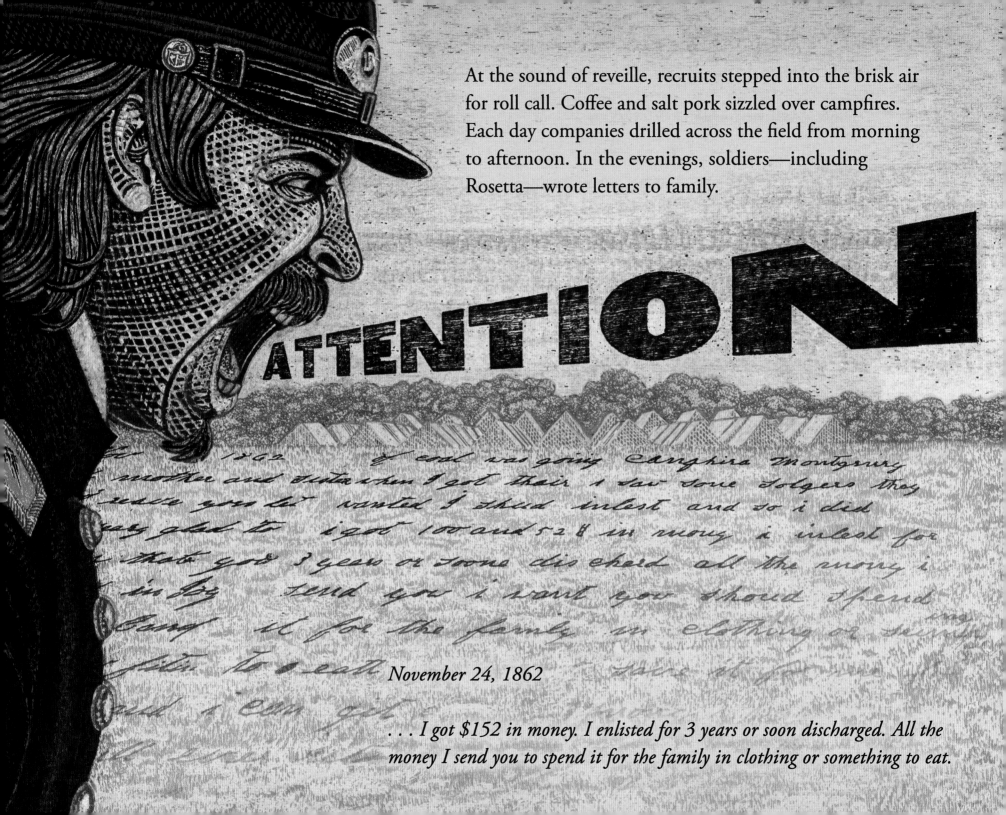

At the sound of reveille, recruits stepped into the brisk air for roll call. Coffee and salt pork sizzled over campfires. Each day companies drilled across the field from morning to afternoon. In the evenings, soldiers—including Rosetta—wrote letters to family.

*November 24, 1862*

*. . . I got $152 in money. I enlisted for 3 years or soon discharged. All the money I send you to spend it for the family in clothing or something to eat.*

...to see than him...

...sword like ter be used...

Some of our men has been...
furnished very bad that for...
my part I shan't been...
I wished times I never...
in the swamps I never got...
to frighten but give...
Mr Stephen Wiley...
on me and I give...
at home prity good...
and he poot down...
with him self as for...
home I shall come...
live long enough...
look for me untill...
me whaire zow aire...

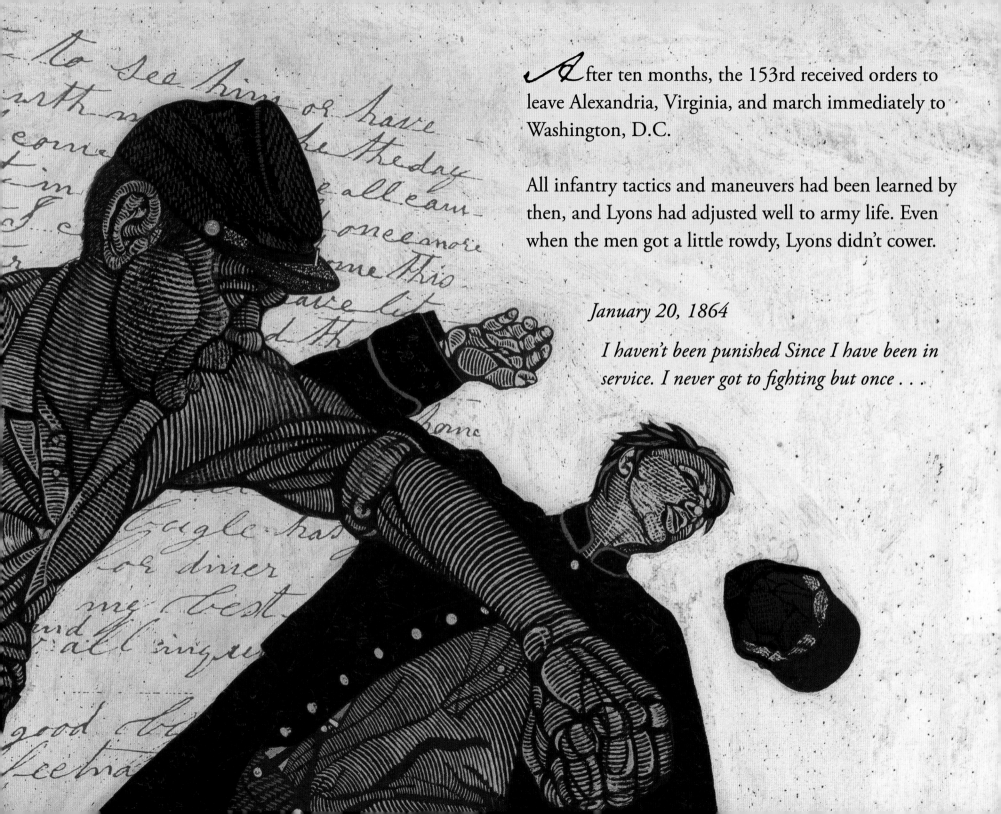

After ten months, the 153rd received orders to leave Alexandria, Virginia, and march immediately to Washington, D.C.

All infantry tactics and maneuvers had been learned by then, and Lyons had adjusted well to army life. Even when the men got a little rowdy, Lyons didn't cower.

*January 20, 1864*

*I haven't been punished Since I have been in service. I never got to fighting but once . . .*

Lyons and her regiment guarded the city until they received orders to

leave Washington, D.C., to embark on the steamship *Mississippi*.

State of Lou[isiana]
City of [New Orleans]

March the 2 [1841]
Dear Father and Moth[er]
I take the first time
and good gut to rite [know]
and let you know that
I am well wee left
washington the it [Feb]
and marched to alexandr[ia]
wee left alexandria the 20
and I got to new Orleans
the las day of febuary
of algier [we] landed [in] the Citey
on the waterwork on the 24
day out of site of land
from wee shall go
I know near wee shall go
I know wee have [no]

Five men were assigned to each cabin. Each day they steamed farther and farther away from home, as the cabin grew more and more stuffy. But Lyons slept in her uniform to keep her secret safe.

*March 2, 1864*

*. . . I was nine days on the water and six days out of sight of land. Where we shall go from here I don't know . . .*

The steamship *Mississippi* landed at the port of Algiers in Louisiana.
The next day troops headed west by train.

First by rail, then by foot, the 153rd traveled to Franklin City, where they joined a corps of about 20,000 Union soldiers. They continued marching over the next several weeks.

Tramp! Tramp! Tramp! The boys are marching...

$\mathcal{O}$n April 8, 1864, a battle broke out several miles away. Lyons and her regiment remained behind to guard the army supply wagons.

Artillery rumbled from afar until darkness fell. Later that night, the Union army retreated to Pleasant Hill, while the 153rd continued their watch into the night.

Before dawn, the weary soldiers were ordered to join the remaining army.

Confederate skirmishers fired threatening shots from behind the thicket as the 153rd marched along the road by daybreak.

They reached Pleasant Hill sometime before midmorning and prepared themselves for battle. Some pinned their names inside their coats. Some wrote letters to their loved ones, while others prayed.

The Union army began forming their new line of battle.
Lyons stood shoulder to shoulder with her comrades,
ready to face the enemy.

The Confederates attacked with shot and shell. Soon, bullets pierced the air, splintering nearby trees. The ground shook, sending a tremor to Lyons's feet, up to her heart, into her throat. She took aim.

"Load 'em up, boys! Hurry!"

Rattling musketry and popping volleys could be heard through clouds of smoke.

Lyons did not falter under a storm of fire and lead. She held her position, pushing Confederates back.

At midnight, the Union army retreated. They marched without food or water, arriving at Grand Ecore in less than two days. After much needed rest, Lyons wrote one more letter.

*April 14, 1864*

*. . . I was under fire about four hours and laid on the field of battle all night. There was three wounded in my Co. and one killed . . .*

*. . . I feel thankful to God that he spared my life . . .*

. . . *I pray to him that he will lead me safe through the field of battle and that I may return safe home . . .*

I feel thankful
to God that he
spared my life and
gives to him that
he will lead me
through the field of
travel and that I will
return safe thankful
and kind and then
the plea

The war was not over, nor the risk of many more lives. But Lyons remained in the ranks, a place where she longed to be—supporting her family and serving her country.

# GLOSSARY

**American Civil War (1861–1865)** — the war between the northern and southern parts of the United States. Because of disagreements about slavery and its future, eleven states (the South) withdrew from the United States, wanting to become a separate country—the Confederate States of America. The North (the remaining United States) fought to reunify the country and keep the South in the Union.

**Artillery** — large, heavy weapons such as cannons that could shoot explosives at enemy soldiers, equipment, and buildings.

**Blue and Gray** — the colors of the Union army and the Confederate army, respectively. Union soldiers wore blue uniforms, and Confederate soldiers wore gray uniforms. The phrase "blue and gray" was used to represent the two sides of the war.

**Bounty** — a cash bonus paid to encourage men to enlist in the army.

**Coal Barge** — a flat-bottomed ship used to transport coal.

**Companies** — the smallest fighting units for the infantry (soldiers fighting on foot), made up of about 100 soldiers. In the Civil War, companies were grouped together to form regiments or battalions.

**Discharged** — released from military service.

**Drill** — a military exercise repeated in order to train soldiers.

**Dysentery** — a painful, sometimes fatal, disorder of the intestines, characterized by severe diarrhea.

**Enlist** — to volunteer for service in the military.

**Identification Tags** — slips of paper upon which soldiers wrote their names and which they pinned to their uniforms, to identify them in case they were killed in action.

**Musketry** — muskets, a type of front-loaded guns carried by those fighting on foot.

**North** — during the Civil War, the northern part of the United States of America, or the Union.

**Recruits** — newly enlisted members of the military.

**Regiment** — the most basic unit of the Union army for recruiting, training, and moving soldiers.

**Reveille** (pronounced *rev-ah-lee*) — a morning drum roll, bugle call, fife call, or other signal for soldiers to wake up.

**Roll Call (Assembly)** — the time at which a list of names is called to check attendance. In the military, this is often signaled by a bugle call.

**Shell, shot** — an exploding object (like a bullet) fired from guns or cannons.

**Skirmishers** — lightly equipped soldiers responsible for slowing enemy advances.

**South** — during the Civil War, the Confederate States of America, or the Confederacy.

**Steamship** — a ship powered by steam. Both the North and South used steamships to carry troops and supplies.

**Volley** — a military tactic (plan) in which soldiers fire their weapons in the same direction at the same time.

**Woodcut** — an engraving on wood. During the Civil War, the events of a battle—pictured in woodcut form—would usually appear in newspapers two weeks after the action.

# AUTHOR'S NOTE

During my senior illustration semester at the University of Massachusetts Dartmouth in 2000, my artwork showed my interest in women's history. Through my research, I learned of several hundred women who, disguised, served as soldiers during the Civil War. I recall sitting on the library floor, randomly pulling books off the shelf, when I came across *The Uncommon Soldier* by Lauren Cook Burgess.

It ultimately sparked a twelve-year interest, and was my inspiration behind *Guts for Glory*. It was my "aha" moment! I was fascinated by Rosetta's story, and wanted to share it as a picture book biography for children.

Sarah Rosetta Wakeman was born and raised on a farm in Afton, New York, the eldest of nine children. At the age of nineteen she ran away from home dressed as a man. She found work as a canaller, then as a Union private when she enlisted in the 153rd New York State Volunteers in Fonda, New York. Her earnings helped support her family back home. She is the only female soldier whose letters represent a woman's point of view during the Civil War. She survived the Battle of Pleasant Hill on April 9th, 1864, the largest battle west of the Mississippi River, with a combined strength of 24,000 troops. But she would later die from dysentery at age twenty-one. During the Civil War, more soldiers died from disease than from battle wounds.

I began educating myself about the Civil War through readings, videos, audiobooks, and by hand painting miniatures. I created a timeline based on Lyons's (Rosetta's) two-year enlistment, with the interest of retracing her footsteps. I scheduled trips over a two-year period, visting places of interest such as the Chenango Canal in upstate New York, sites around Washington, D.C., and the Mansfield Historic Site Museum and the Pleasant Hill Battle Park. I also attended Civil War reenactments as a spectator. There I discovered a young woman disguised as a soldier. "How cool . . . I could do that, too!" I thought.

I began researching reenactment groups and acquired a uniform and a mail-order reproduction musket. My first attempt to join a reenactment group—disguised as a male soldier—was denied: "Sorry, women soldiers are not authentic to the history of our regiment." My second attempt to join a reenactment group was welcomed by the 22nd Massachusetts Volunteers, a family-oriented reenactment group who accepted disguised female soldiers.

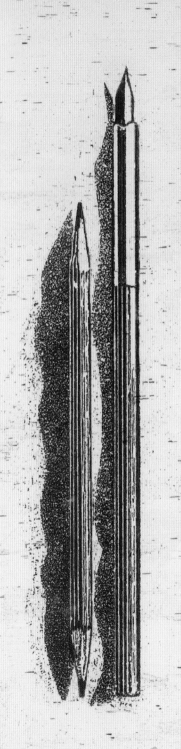

It wasn't customary for a Union soldier to wander freely into Rebel territory, of course. But as a spectator at reenactments, I was able to visit Confederate camps up close and personal. I also had the chance to watch mock battles from a distance, which helped me get a panoramic sense of the chaos of battle.

When I joined the reenactments, I placed myself in a Union private's experience, from the taste of black powder from tearing open a blank cartridge with my teeth, or the deafening pop from a fired musket, the smell of a discharged rifle, to the singe of a barrel, too hot to touch. I believe the six years of reenacting enhanced my writing and illustrating of *Guts for Glory*.

I never expected to have an interest in the Civil War. Rosetta's story inspired me to follow my own path. I hope *Guts for Glory* helps you discover yours.

## ABOUT THE ART

I composed the illustrations in scratchboard, which, like the wood engravings of the nineteenth century, uses an engraver or knife to cut a surface and create images. Instead of cutting designs into wood, scratchboard art scrapes ink off the surface of a board. I made most of the boards myself by airbrushing Japanese sumi ink onto either illustration or commercial posterboard to convey a gritty and difficult time in American history. I used premade boards to capture the finer details of the ambrotype (early photo) spots and the wallpapered full-page spread where Rosetta disguises herself.

The drawings were transferred onto the inked boards with tracing and carbon paper. The images were scratched using an X-Acto knife #11 blade, a utility blade for the large white areas, and steel wool to replicate the texture of a Union soldier's wool uniform. The black areas (inked) remained intact (positive spaces), while the white areas (negative spaces) were scratched out. The whole process is like drawing in reverse. Scratchboard is forgiving, where mistakes can be re-inked and re-scratched. White areas can be painted in with white acrylic paint for touch-up. Then the finished images were scanned, spliced, and digitally colored. Revising was constant through every phase of the book. Each spread was researched based on its specific subject, from Rosetta's work dress, a gentleman's cravat (necktie), the whippletree mechanism from a two-mule team, to the true-to-scale paraphernalia found on the endsheets.

# MORE ABOUT ROSETTA WAKEMAN AND THE CIVIL WAR

### A Nation Divided in Two

From 1861 to 1865, the United States fought a war against itself—the bloodiest war in American history. Since the founding of the United States, its people had argued about slavery and the role of government in its future. Tensions rose for decades, until eleven states decided to secede (withdraw) from the United States and become a separate country: the Confederate States of America. When the Confederacy fired on Fort Sumter in South Carolina in April 1861, the Civil War officially began. The fighting would continue for over four years, during which over 620,000 soldiers would die (sometimes in battle, but usually of disease). When the North finally won in 1865, the Union had been preserved—and thousands of Americans had been changed by the realities of war.

### Women in the Civil War

In the 1860s, women could not vote, run for political office, or enlist in the army, but they still longed to shape the outcome of the Civil War. On the home front, women grew crops, sewed clothing, gathered money and supplies, and worked jobs that men had filled before they left for the war. But many women longed to be closer to the battlefield. Risking social scandal, they volunteered for difficult and sometimes dangerous roles. Some—like Dorothea Dix, Dr. Mary Walker, and Susie King Taylor—helped the sick and wounded. Others—like Harriet Tubman, Elizabeth Van Lew, and Mary Jane Richards—acted as spies and smugglers. And some—like Frances Louisa Clayton, Mary Ann Clark, and Rosetta Wakeman—disguised themselves as men and enlisted in the army.

*Rosetta "Lyons" Wakeman in uniform, c. 1862*

### A Woman in the Ranks

Historians estimate that hundreds of women served as soldiers in the Civil War. Though neither the Union nor Confederate army allowed women to officially enlist, letters and other historical sources reveal female soldiers in both armies who chose to serve through secrecy. Each woman had her own reasons for joining: to fight for her beliefs, to find adventure and independence, to stay with a husband or brother, to make more money than she could in a woman's job. Though some women's disguises were discovered before they could join the army, many— like Rosetta—slipped into the ranks without raising suspicion.

If a soldier was found to be female, she could be discharged for "sexual incompatibility": being the wrong sex to serve in the military. But in the early 1860s, no one carried official, government-issued identification cards. Army staff and medical examiners rarely asked more than a few questions about a recruit's background. In the camps, most soldiers bathed privately and slept in their loose, ill-fitting uniforms. Strict Victorian social dress codes meant that very few men had ever seen a woman wearing anything but a dress and long hair. As long as a female soldier didn't act too strangely and didn't need major medical attention, she could often serve undetected for years.

### A Life in the Army

For Rosetta and her comrades in the Union army, most days would have fallen into repetitive routines. While in Alexandria, Virginia, and Washington, D.C., Rosetta and the 153rd regiment's duties included running military drills, practicing marching, and guarding Carroll Prison on Capitol Hill. Back in camp, soldiers played games and instruments, read books and newspapers, and wrote letters home to their friends and family. The postal service delivered thousands of letters during the Civil War, often at free or discounted prices for Union soldiers. Over 90 percent of the army could read and write, and those who could not (like many formerly enslaved Black soldiers) sometimes learned how in army camps. These thousands of writers—including Rosetta—shared news from the front and asked for news from home. We have no records of what the Wakemans thought of their soldier-daughter's letters as they arrived, but (however they felt) they stored her letters for years after the war. Rosetta wrote frequently, constantly reassuring her family that she was still well.

But for soldiers, exhaustion and fear were never far away. Steamship journeys could take days or weeks. Once on land, regiments marched miles on foot for long, hot hours through forests and swamps. In battle, soldiers faced more explosive dangers—from bullets to grapeshot and other cannon fire. Even after combat ended, the threat of illness and infection remained. Over 400,000 soldiers (two-thirds of the total Civil War deaths) died of disease, not battle wounds. Because of unsanitary conditions, millions of soldiers suffered from diarrhea, dysentery, malaria, typhoid, and pneumonia. For those like Rosetta, hospitalization carried an additional risk: the possibility of discovery.

## A Legacy in Letters

On June 19, 1864, Rosetta Wakeman died from dysentery—the deadliest disease of the Civil War—at Marine USA General Hospital in New Orleans, Louisiana. Rosetta had been hospitalized for over a month, and during that time (as far as history records), no one had learned her secret. She was buried under the name Lyons Wakeman in Chalmette National Cemetery. Those who knew kept her secret, and Rosetta's much-younger sister Catherine grew up thinking her older brother—not sister—had served. Through the efforts of Catherine and other relatives,

Rosetta's letters were eventually published as the only letters that share a woman soldier's perspective on the Civil War as it happened.

Because Rosetta died during the war, we cannot know what choices she would have made after it ended, and we cannot know whether she would have spoken publicly about her experiences. After the Civil War, similar soldiers made very different decisions about how to live and how to tell their stories. Lucy Gauss Kenney, who fought as Bill Thompson, only revealed her secret decades later in 1914. Sarah Emma Edmonds, who served as Franklin Thompson, published a book about her experiences and became the only female member of the Grand Army of the Republic (a veterans' organization). Albert D. J. Cashier, who was born Jennie Hodgers, lived as a man for over fifty years after the war ended, and many people today consider him an example of a transgender man in history.

During her service, Rosetta used the names Lyons Wakeman and Edwin Wakeman, sometimes signing her letters as Lyons, sometimes as Edwin, and sometimes as Rosetta. In one letter, she signed "Rosetta"

*Rosetta "Lyons" Wakeman's tombstone, near New Orleans, LA*

and then wrote "Edwin" over it. Her ring is engraved with the words "Rosetta Wakeman / Co. H / 153rd N.Y. Vol." To reflect historical details like these, and to help readers track Rosetta's story, this book uses female pronouns for Rosetta throughout and refers to her as "Lyons" during her time in the army. The endnotes, for consistency, use "Rosetta." We are deeply grateful for Rosetta's letters, which allow us to meet this fascinating, complicated person of the past through her own words.

# A TIMELINE OF EVENTS

**1843**

**January 16, 1843** — Sarah Rosetta Wakeman is born near modern-day Afton Township, New York, the oldest of nine children born to Harvey Anable Wakeman and Emily Hale Wakeman.

**1860**

**1860** — The 1860 census reports Rosetta as seventeen years old and having attended some school in the past year.

**December 1860 – February 1861** — Seven US states break away from the Union and form the Confederate States of America with Jefferson Davis as president. A total of eleven states will eventually secede (withdraw) from the Union to join the Confederacy.

**1861**

**April 12–13, 1861** — The Civil War begins when the Confederacy fires on Fort Sumter in South Carolina.

**July 21, 1861** — The first major battle of the Civil War—a shocking Union loss—is fought at the stream of Bull Run, near the town of Manassas in Virginia.

**1862**

**July 1862** — After a discouraging lack of progress in the war, US President Abraham Lincoln calls for state governors to recruit 300,000 more volunteers for the Union army.

**August 1862** — At age nineteen, Rosetta leaves home disguised as "Lyons" Wakeman and begins working on the Chenango Canal. On August 30, Lyons Wakeman enrolls in the 153rd Regiment of the New York State Volunteers.

**October 18, 1862** — The 153rd leaves New York state for Alexandria, Virginia, where they will assist with the defenses of Washington, D.C., and train for battle.

**1863**

**January 1, 1863** — President Abraham Lincoln issues the Emancipation Proclamation, which declares that all people enslaved in Confederate states are now free. As a result, many Black soldiers join the Union army. "They have drafted a good many men in Washington," Rosetta writes later in 1863. "They have drafted black men as well as White men."

**July 20, 1863** — The 153rd is transferred to Washington, D.C., and moves into barracks on Capitol Hill. On August 5, Rosetta writes a letter to her family describing the US Capitol and its dome, which is currently under construction: "I have been inside of it . . . That is a pretty place you better believe."

**1864**

**February 20–29, 1864** — The 153rd sails on the steamship *Mississippi* to Algiers, Louisiana. Once in the South, they march for miles on foot (sometimes eighteen miles per day) to join the Union army's Red River Campaign.

**March 10, 1864** — About 30,000 Union soldiers, under the command of Major General Nathaniel P. Banks, begin the Red River Campaign, an attempt to capture Shreveport, Louisiana (the capital of Confederate Louisiana), and cut off Confederate resources.

**April 9, 1864** — Rosetta participates in the Battle of Pleasant Hill, the largest battle west of the Mississippi River and the last major battle of the Red River Campaign's Louisiana phase. The Battle of Mansfield—a Confederate victory—had been fought the previous day. Though the Union technically wins the Battle of Pleasant Hill, the Union army is forced to retreat.

**April 14, 1864** — Rosetta writes her final letter home: "I feel thankful to God that he spared my life and I pray to him that he will lead me safe through the field of battle and that I may return safe home."

**May 3, 1864** — Rosetta is admitted to the 153rd Regimental Hospital, suffering from dysentery—the most deadly disease of the Civil War.

**May 21, 1864** — After a series of Union failures, the Red River Campaign is abandoned.

**June 19, 1864** — After over a month of hospitalization, Rosetta dies at Marine USA General Hospital in New Orleans, Louisiana. She is buried at Chalmette National Cemetery in New Orleans under her enlisted name Lyons Wakeman.

**July 1, 1864** — The 153rd heads to Washington, D.C., where they will help defend Fort Stevens, and then join Major General Philip Sheridan's Shenandoah Valley campaign. They will eventually return to Washington, D.C., and serve there until after the end of the war.

**1865**

**April 9, 1865** — After a long, grueling series of Union victories and Confederate losses, Confederate General Robert E. Lee surrenders to Union General Ulysses S. Grant at Appomattox Court House, Virginia. By July, all Confederate armies have surrendered. The Civil War ends.

**October 2, 1865** — After four months stationed in Georgia, the 153rd regiment sends its soldiers home. During its service, the 153rd has lost 200 soldiers—20 percent of its officers and enlistees—to battle wounds or disease.

# ROSETTA WAKEMAN'S LETTERS (1862–1864)

*Rosetta Wakeman is the only female Civil War soldier whose wartime letters (dated from November 1862 to April 1864)
are known to have survived into the present. Below are longer versions of the letters quoted in this book.*

Alexandria, VA
November 24, 1862

My Dear Father and mother and sister and brothers, one in all, . . .

I got $152 in money. I enlisted for 3 years or soon discharged. All the money I send you to spend it for the family in clothing or something to eat. Don't save it for me for I can get all the money I want. If I ever return I shall have money enough for my self and to divide with you . . . I want to drop all old affray [fighting] and I want you to do the same and when i come home we will be good friends as ever.

Capitol Hill,
Washington, D.C.
January 20, 1864

Dear Father,

. . . Some of our men have been punished very bad, but for my part I haven't been punished Since I have been in service. I never got to fighting but once. Then Mr. Stephen Wiley pitched on me and I give him three or four pretty good cracks . . . I hope the day will come when we all can meet in this world once more but I can't come home this winter, for they have let some go home and they haven't come back yet.

State of Louisiana,
City of Algiers
March 2, 1864

Dear Father and Mother,

I take the first time I could get to write to you and let you know that I am well. We left washington the 18 of feb. and marched to Alexandria. We left Alexandria the 20 and got to new Orleans the last day of february. We landed in the City of Algiers the 29 of day of february. I was nine days on the water and six days out of sight of land. Where we shall go from here I don't know . . .

Grand Ecore Landing, LA
Red River
April 14, 1864

Dear Mother, Father, Brothers and Sisters,

Our army made an advance up the river to pleasant hill about 40 miles. There we had a fight . . . The next day I had to face the enemy bullets with my regiment. I was under fire about four hours and laid on the field of battle all night. There was three wounded in my Co. and one killed . . .

I feel thankful to God that he spared my life and I pray to him that he will lead me safe through the field of battle and that I may return safe home . . .

# ENDPAPER GLOSSARY

*Use the information below to identify the true-to-scale items on the following pages that Civil War soldiers like Rosetta would have carried with them.*

1. **Sowbelly (Salt Pork)** — Most common meat issued to Northern soldiers. Daily ration of twelve ounces.

2. **Hardtack** — A hard biscuit made of flour, water, and salt. Daily ration of nine crackers (16 ounces).

3. **Coffee** — Raw whole (green) bean coffee for roasting and drinking.

4. **Bone Toothbrush** — With pig hair bristles.

5. **Inkwell** — Eight-sided umbrella ink bottle made of blown glass.

6. **Lantern Candle** — Most commonly made from tallow, beeswax, or adamantine. Soldiers also used commercially made stearin candles, often called "star" candles because of Proctor & Gamble's popular "Star Candle" stearin line.

7. **Ration Soap** — Made from ash, animal fat, lye (sodium hydroxide), and water. Harsh on skin.

8. **Ration Comb** — Made of animal bone and used especially to comb out hair lice.

9. **Dip Pen** — Wooden handle with steel nib to dip into ink. When writing, the pen needed to be dipped into ink every few lines.

10. **Paper Cartridge** — A rolled paper tube charge of sixty-five grains of black powder and .58 caliber bullet.

11. **Williams Type II Cleaner Bullet** — Helped reduce gunpowder buildup by scraping the muzzle with zinc disc. Used to load muskets.

12. **Minié Ball** — .58 caliber musket bullet.

13. **Musket Worm (Wiper 59 caliber)** — Screwed onto bottom of ramrod (a steel rod used to pack the bullet down the musket barrel). Includes cloth patches for cleaning the musket barrel of gunpowder residue.

14. **Ball Puller .58 Caliber (Bell-Screw)** — Screwed onto bottom of ramrod for extracting dislodged bullet.

15. **Tompion** — Made of wood or cork placed in muzzle to keep out moisture.

16. **Arsenal Pack** — Paper wrapper contained nine .58 caliber paper bullet cartridges, one .58 caliber Williams Type II (cleaner bullet) paper cartridge, and one paper cartridge of twelve percussion caps.

17. **Musket Wrench** — Combination wrench and screwdriver used to remove the firing cone and dismantle the lock.

18. **Firing Cone** — Ignites spark through gunpowder charge when musket hammer strikes percussion cap, which helps the gun fire.

19. **Percussion Caps** — Paper-wrapped package of twelve brass or copper percussion caps containing a small amount of mercury fulminate. When the musket was fired, the hammer struck the cap over the firing cone, sending a spark to the gunpowder charge and detonating the bullet.

20. **Cone (Wire) Picker** — Used to clean the firing cone of gunpowder residue.

21. **Pocket Knife**